Short Vowels, oo, ee, final e, ea, ai, oa

This book belongs to

_____

COPYRIGHT © 2015 Nanci Bell
Gander Publishing
P.O. Box 780
Avila Beach, CA 93424
805-541-5523 • 800-554-1819

SEEING STARS IS A REGISTERED TRADEMARK OF NANCI BELL.

All rights reserved. No part of this material shall be reproduced or transmitted in any form or by any means, electronic or mechanical, including photocopying, recording, or by any information or retrieval system, without prior written permission from the Publisher. Printed in the U.S.A.

18 17 16 15   1 2 3 4

ISBN 978-1-935596-61-5

Overview and Directions

Seeing Stars® CVC Easy Decoding Workbooks are supplementary to the *Seeing Stars* program. The goal is to develop *decoding skills* and stimulate symbol imagery as a primary sensory-cognitive function necessary for monitoring, self-correction, and fluency in reading and spelling tasks.

Each workbook provides specific practice in

- decoding nonwords and real words to improve word attack skills,
- reading sight words to improve word recognition skills and fluency,
- reading stories to apply sight words and contextual guessing to context, and
- visualizing stories for language comprehension.

Simple Syllables and 90 Star (Sight) Words:

The *CVC Easy Decoding Workbooks* provide the student with the opportunity for lots of decoding and sight word practice. The workbooks progress sequentially—easiest, easier, and easy. The letters at the top of each page are referencing the phoneme; for example, a equals /a/, as in pat.

- EASY DECODING A: Short vowels: a, e, i, o, u, and Star Words 1-30
- EASY DECODING B: Short vowels, oo, ee, and final e, and Star Words 31-60
- EASY DECODING C: Short vowels, oo, ee, final e, ea, ai, oa, and Star Words 61-90

Decode, Decode, Decode the Reading List:

Students need to decode, decode, decode—and there are 680 words in each workbook!

- There are twenty words in each Reading List to provide your student with practice decoding both nonwords and real words. Along with decoding, at times use the words to stimulate your student's symbol imagery. For example: *"Read the word. Now cover it…and air-write it. What is the fourth letter you picture?"*

- The heading at the top of each page indicates the phonetic processing for that lesson. "CVC, short vowels, one change" means the Reading List will have CVC patterns with short vowels (shorts) and one sound changing at a time—lap, lip, lit, etc.

- The structure of the syllable is based on phonology, not letters. For example, "will" is a CVC pattern because it has three phonemes, despite the four letters.

- I included nonwords in the reading lists to stimulate phonetic processing. Since memory and/or oral vocabulary cannot aid his word reading, your student has to accurately decode—guessing won't work.

- If a nonword can be spelled differently to make a real word—teach it accurately. For example, decoding the nonword "ame" prepares students for reading words such as "tame" and "same." But "ame" is misspelled! So rather than leave your student with an inaccurate visual imprint for the word, show him the real way to spell "aim" and help him create a mental representation for the meaning: *"The word 'aim' is spelled like this. See it and write it in the air. Here's what you can picture for the meaning of the word 'aim.'"*

The Blank Spelling List:

Use the blank spaces on the Spelling List to have your student spell words appropriate to the phonological and orthographic patterns presented on the page. Do not have him spell the exact same words he just read on the Reading List of that page! Instead, use words from a previous list, make up your own, use Star Words from that page, or use his spelling list from school. Most important, if decoding is your focus, don't have your student spell all ten words. Instead, have him read twenty and spell five. Remember, decode, decode, decode!

The Little Gray Line and Keeping Score:

Use the little gray lines in front of the Reading List and Spelling List to mark a plus (+) when your student decodes the word accurately. If your student has self-corrected, circle the number and then mark a plus. For the total correct, only count the words he decoded accurately the first time. Sometimes it is helpful to have your student say the vowel before he reads the word: *"Touch the vowel, say the sound, and then read the word."*

The scores for reading and spelling enable you and your student to track progress. You can both see improvement if you look back and see 5/20 has now improved to 18/20 or 20/20. The end of the workbook has a place for you to note observations so you can prescribe and pace appropriately.

Stimulate Imagery for Star Word Memorization:

These workbooks provide reading and spelling practice and also the opportunity for symbol imagery stimulation. Symbol imagery is orthographic awareness and the necessary sensory input for rapid self-correction—reading fluency requires this rapid self-correction.

Reading fluency also requires a well-established sight word vocabulary and each workbook offers lots of opportunity for sight word practice. Sets of ten Star Words are repeated for ten pages each, giving your student lots of exposure to the words.

At times have your student air-write a word after he decodes it. Then ask specific questions, such as *"What was the second letter you saw?"* Remember to question to phonological irregularities (have, been, etc.) so the irregularity can be placed in his orthographic memory.

The Little Stories:

The little stories give your student the opportunity to apply his decoding to contextual reading fluency—but they also offer the opportunity to develop concept imagery and occasionally contextual guessing.

- Have your student tell you what he visualizes for the story: *"What did those words make you picture?"*
- Toward the end of some stories, I included an unfamiliar word(s) to give your student the opportunity to use his decoding and concept imagery to make a reasonable guess based on context. If he struggles, tell the word(s) to him.
- While these are essentially decoding workbooks, I included sentence writing so your student would have a full experience with written language. Students write a sentence every six pages, using a word or two from the Star Word list.

Group Stimulation:

The workbooks are used for both individual and group practice. Each student should have a book. In small groups or whole classrooms, all students respond to your instruction. Call on a student to read a specific word and keep others involved by signaling agreement or not, as in, *"Buzz, read number three, and say the vowel first. The rest of you, give thumbs up or down."*

For spelling, say the word to be spelled, then call on a student to spell it aloud: *"Buzz, tell us how you spelled the word 'pip.' Thumbs up or down, everyone? Now let's all spell it in the air."*

For sentence reading or spelling, simply take turns and then discuss the concept imagery. Easy!

1 CVC short vowels (shorts) and final e (one change)

Date:_____

Reading Score: /20		Spelling Score: /10	Star Words (61 through 70)
1. rag	11. sog	1. _____	1. **her**
2. gag	12. gog	2. _____	2. **some**
3. gig	13. jog	3. _____	3. **has**
4. jig	14. jot	4. _____	4. **him**
5. mig	15. jet	5. _____	5. **these**
6. mag	16. met	6. _____	6. **look**
7. tag	17. mat	7. _____	7. **like**
8. sag	18. mate	8. _____	8. **make**
9. seg	19. tate	9. _____	9. **time**
10. sug	20. tape	10. _____	10. **then**

Read and picture this little story:

I will make time to see her. I will make time to see him. Then I will see them. We will have some fun at the beach.

2. CVC

shorts, ee, and final e (one change)

Date: _____

Reading Score: __/20

1. chap
2. chip
3. ship
4. Shep
5. sheep
6. cheep
7. jeep
8. jeeth
9. teeth
10. tath
11. math
12. mash
13. mag
14. nag
15. nog
16. nod
17. node
18. chode
19. chide
20. bide

Spelling Score: __/10

1. _____
2. _____
3. _____
4. _____
5. _____
6. _____
7. _____
8. _____
9. _____
10. _____

Star Words (61 through 70)

1. **has**
2. **like**
3. **these**
4. **her**
5. **time**
6. **him**
7. **then**
8. **some**
9. **make**
10. **look**

Read and picture this little story:

Jack can ride in his red jeep. He can do his math in his red jeep. He can sleep in his red jeep. He can do all these things in his fun red jeep.

3. CVC

shorts, ee, and oo (one change)

Date:_____

Reading Score: __/20

1. seek
2. keek
3. meek
4. meet
5. mat
6. moot
7. boot
8. loot
9. let
10. led
11. lud
12. lad
13. lan
14. loon
15. noon
16. nun
17. fun
18. shun
19. sheen
20. sheep

Spelling Score: __/10

1. _____
2. _____
3. _____
4. _____
5. _____
6. _____
7. _____
8. _____
9. _____
10. _____

Star Words (61 through 70)

1. **some**
2. **these**
3. **has**
4. **time**
5. **her**
6. **make**
7. **then**
8. **look**
9. **him**
10. **like**

Read and picture this little story:

The sheep has big big big teeth. He can bite with these big white teeth. He can eat with his big white teeth. His teeth can do some good things for him.

4 CVC shorts, oo, and ee (one change)

Date: _____

Reading   Score: __/20

1. boon
2. ban
3. bun
4. Ben
5. ten
6. teen
7. keen
8. sheen
9. shoon
10. Shan
11. Jan
12. Jack
13. cack
14. lack
15. lat
16. lit
17. lut
18. let
19. loot
20. looj

Spelling   Score: __/10

1. _____
2. _____
3. _____
4. _____
5. _____
6. _____
7. _____
8. _____
9. _____
10. _____

Star Words
(61 through 70)

1. **make**
2. **like**
3. **time**
4. **then**
5. **has**
6. **look**
7. **some**
8. **her**
9. **him**
10. **these**

Read and picture this little story:

Mom has some little boots. Her little boots are white. Dad has some big red boots. Dad can kick high with his red boots.

5 CVC

shorts, oo, and ee
(one and multi-change)

Date:_____

Reading Score: __/20

1. vat
2. vet
3. vut
4. roof
5. rof
6. rot
7. hot
8. chot
9. shot
10. sheet
11. shut
12. shoot
13. din
14. rub
15. bath
16. booth
17. chip
18. gap
19. gal
20. room

Spelling Score: __/10

1. _____
2. _____
3. _____
4. _____
5. _____
6. _____
7. _____
8. _____
9. _____
10. _____

Star Words
(31 through 40)

1. **look**
2. **him**
3. **has**
4. **make**
5. **time**
6. **then**
7. **some**
8. **like**
9. **these**
10. **her**

Read and picture this little story:

I will meet you, then we will have some time to eat. We can not meet on the moon. We can not meet on the roof. But we can meet in the shop and I can make your food.

6 CVC
shorts, ee, and final e (multi-change)

Date: _____

Reading Score: __/20

- 1. tub
- 2. Nate
- 3. roop
- 4. peel
- 5. zap
- 6. dot
- 7. hid
- 8. rash
- 9. bab
- 10. beek
- 11. shot
- 12. mam
- 13. lash
- 14. mush
- 15. shame
- 16. chum
- 17. hash
- 18. his
- 19. bam
- 20. jog

Spelling Score: __/10

1. _____
2. _____
3. _____
4. _____
5. _____
6. _____
7. _____
8. _____
9. _____
10. _____

Star Words
(61 through 70)

1. **these**
2. **time**
3. **look**
4. **like**
5. **some**
6. **her**
7. **then**
8. **make**
9. **has**
10. **him**

★ *Write* We can not meet on the roof.

_____

_____

7 CVC

shorts and ea (one change)

Date:_____

Reading Score: __/20

1. beat
2. meat
3. seat
4. set
5. let
6. lef
7. leaf
8. leap
9. lap
10. lan
11. lean
12. leam
13. team
14. teach
15. peach
16. reach
17. real
18. seal
19. sell
20. tell

Spelling Score: __/10

1. _____
2. _____
3. _____
4. _____
5. _____
6. _____
7. _____
8. _____
9. _____
10. _____

Star Words
(61 through 70)

1. **then**
2. **these**
3. **her**
4. **time**
5. **like**
6. **make**
7. **some**
8. **him**
9. **has**
10. **look**

Read and picture this little story:

I like to eat meat in my seat. I like to eat a peach in my seat. I do not like to eat a leaf in my seat. I may have to pick a leaf from my teeth!

8 CVC

shorts, ee, final e, and ea (one change)

Date: _____

Reading Score: __/20

1. Jean
2. lean
3. Len
4. Ian
5. lap
6. leap
7. zeap
8. zeep
9. zepe
10. zap
11. chap
12. cheep
13. cheap
14. heap
15. hup
16. hub
17. sub
18. sib
19. sibe
20. site

Spelling Score: __/10

1. _____
2. _____
3. _____
4. _____
5. _____
6. _____
7. _____
8. _____
9. _____
10. _____

Star Words
(61 through 70)

1. **has**
2. **her**
3. **time**
4. **look**
5. **some**
6. **him**
7. **then**
8. **like**
9. **these**
10. **make**

Read and picture this little story:

Buzz had a pet seal and his name was Sun Tan. Sun Tan liked to look at the moon. Sun Tan liked to look at the sun. Sun Tan and Buzz liked to catch his red ball.

9 CVC

shorts, ee, final e, and ea
(one change)

Date: _____

Reading Score: __/20

1. cub
2. cube
3. cute
4. cut
5. cat
6. Cate
7. mate
8. meat
9. meet
10. meef
11. reef
12. reaf
13. reach
14. ream
15. team
16. tam
17. tame
18. same
19. Sam
20. Sal

Spelling Score: __/10

1. _____
2. _____
3. _____
4. _____
5. _____
6. _____
7. _____
8. _____
9. _____
10. _____

Star Words
(61 through 70)

1. **like**
2. **make**
3. **her**
4. **some**
5. **him**
6. **look**
7. **then**
8. **has**
9. **these**
10. **time**

Read and picture this little story:

My dog has the same name as my cat. His name is Sam and my cat's name is Sam too. Sometimes I call, "Sam!" and my cat runs to me. My dog, Sam, can get very mad at my cat!

10 CVC

shorts, oo, final e, and ea
(one and multi-change)

Date: _____

Reading Score: __/20

1. name
2. tab
3. cool
4. jazz
5. chat
6. whig
7. cove
8. mum
9. fume
10. wife
11. tale
12. teal
13. fish
14. leach
15. moss
16. naze
17. gum
18. deal
19. whim
20. gut

Spelling Score: __/10

1. _____
2. _____
3. _____
4. _____
5. _____
6. _____
7. _____
8. _____
9. _____
10. _____

Star Words
(61 through 70)

1. **time**
2. **look**
3. **these**
4. **then**
5. **make**
6. **some**
7. **like**
8. **her**
9. **has**
10. **him**

Read and picture this little story:

Jack's team will love to have fun at the zoo. They will go to the zoo and see the big lions. They will go to the zoo and see the big elephants. They will go to the zoo and eat candy!

11 CVC

shorts, final e, and ea
(one and multi-change)

Date:_____

Reading Score: /20

1. sat
2. nef
3. mean
4. win
5. hide
6. cut
7. gas
8. dean
9. fog
10. toss
11. Dan
12. sis
13. ham
14. late
15. heap
16. note
17. bean
18. them
19. lag
20. whip

Spelling Score: /10

1. _____
2. _____
3. _____
4. _____
5. _____
6. _____
7. _____
8. _____
9. _____
10. _____

Star Words
(71 through 80)

1. **more**
2. **two**
3. **now**
4. **been**
5. **long**
6. **than**
7. **write**
8. **did**
9. **sit**
10. **down**

Read and picture this little story:

Mike has one dog and two cats. Jack has two cats and one dog. Then they came to play with each other. Now Mike and Jack had six pets!

12 CVC

shorts, ee, and ea
(one change)

Date: _____

Reading Score: __/20

1. meal
2. mean
3. man
4. mad
5. mead
6. read
7. red
8. Jed
9. jead
10. Jean
11. Jen
12. jep
13. jeep
14. cheep
15. cheap
16. cheat
17. heat
18. wheat
19. wet
20. well

Spelling Score: __/10

1. _____
2. _____
3. _____
4. _____
5. _____
6. _____
7. _____
8. _____
9. _____
10. _____

Star Words
(71 through 80)

1. **two**
2. **now**
3. **than**
4. **did**
5. **write**
6. **more**
7. **long**
8. **down**
9. **sit**
10. **been**

★ *Write* Jack has two cats and one dog.

13 CVC

shorts, ee, final e, and ea
(one and multi-change)

Date:_____

Reading   Score: __/20

1. lean
2. nap
3. zeat
4. cheap
5. cheek
6. check
7. chick
8. lick
9. sick
10. sack
11. meek
12. lape
13. late
14. real
15. lip
16. lep
17. lup
18. luck
19. theme
20. read

Spelling   Score: __/10

1. _____
2. _____
3. _____
4. _____
5. _____
6. _____
7. _____
8. _____
9. _____
10. _____

Star Words
(71 through 80)

1. **now**
2. **than**
3. **down**
4. **did**
5. **sit**
6. **two**
7. **write**
8. **been**
9. **more**
10. **long**

Read and picture this little story:

Nan likes to write for fun. She can sit down and write and write. She can write more and more and more. Soon she has lots and lots of stories.

14 CVC

shorts, ea, and ai
(one change)

Date:_____

Reading Score: /20

- 1. pain
- 2. pan
- 3. pad
- 4. paid
- 5. maid
- 6. mad
- 7. mid
- 8. mill
- 9. meal
- 10. mail
- 11. sail
- 12. rail
- 13. pail
- 14. tail
- 15. till
- 16. tin
- 17. tain
- 18. rain
- 19. rin
- 20. chin

Spelling Score: /10

- 1. _____
- 2. _____
- 3. _____
- 4. _____
- 5. _____
- 6. _____
- 7. _____
- 8. _____
- 9. _____
- 10. _____

Star Words
(71 through 80)

1. **write**
2. **two**
3. **been**
4. **now**
5. **sit**
6. **long**
7. **down**
8. **more**
9. **than**
10. **did**

Read and picture this little story:

Mick had been sick. He had been sick for a long time. Then he ate some good food. Soon he was well and happy.

15 CVC

shorts, final e, ea, and ai (one change)

Date:_____

Reading Score: /20

1. mail
2. sail
3. fail
4. fain
5. fan
6. fat
7. fate
8. fame
9. same
10. lame
11. tame
12. tam
13. Tim
14. tem
15. tum
16. sum
17. seam
18. team
19. tam
20. tack

Spelling Score: /10

1. _____
2. _____
3. _____
4. _____
5. _____
6. _____
7. _____
8. _____
9. _____
10. _____

Star Words
(71 through 80)

1. **down**
2. **write**
3. **two**
4. **did**
5. **more**
6. **been**
7. **now**
8. **than**
9. **sit**
10. **long**

Read and picture this little story:

I had a sack of leeks. I gave them to my mom to cook for me. But she was not home. I put the leeks in my cheeks and then I got sick.

16 CVC — shorts, final e, ea, and ai (one and multi-change)

Date: _____

Reading   Score: __/20

1. wait
2. fill
3. neck
4. neat
5. beat
6. sail
7. tail
8. fail
9. nail
10. nick
11. rail
12. real
13. fell
14. sell
15. sack
16. fame
17. mail
18. meal
19. zeal
20. chill

Spelling   Score: __/10

1. _____
2. _____
3. _____
4. _____
5. _____
6. _____
7. _____
8. _____
9. _____
10. _____

Star Words (71 through 80)

1. **been**
2. **now**
3. **down**
4. **long**
5. **did**
6. **sit**
7. **more**
8. **than**
9. **write**
10. **two**

Read and picture this little story:

Mack and Mick can sail a ship. They can sail for a long time. They do it more and more. Soon they will live on their ship.

17 CVC

shorts, final e, ea, ai, and oa (one change)

Date: _____

Reading Score: /20

1. soap
2. soak
3. soat
4. boat
5. beat
6. bait
7. gait
8. goat
9. gat
10. gate
11. rate
12. rat
13. rad
14. road
15. toad
16. tead
17. Ted
18. toad
19. load
20. lad

Spelling Score: /10

1. _____
2. _____
3. _____
4. _____
5. _____
6. _____
7. _____
8. _____
9. _____
10. _____

Star Words (71 through 80)

1. **did**
2. **more**
3. **than**
4. **two**
5. **been**
6. **long**
7. **down**
8. **write**
9. **sit**
10. **now**

Read and picture this little story:

Shan had a long tail. She had a long nose. She had long ears. Now what is Shan?

18 CVC

a mix of everything!
(one change)

Date:_____

Reading Score: /20

1. chain
2. chean
3. cheat
4. heat
5. heap
6. leap
7. lap
8. lat
9. late
10. loat
11. moat
12. foat
13. fat
14. fate
15. hate
16. hat
17. bat
18. bait
19. bit
20. bite

Spelling Score: /10

1. _____
2. _____
3. _____
4. _____
5. _____
6. _____
7. _____
8. _____
9. _____
10. _____

Star Words
(71 through 80)

1. **more**
2. **down**
3. **long**
4. **than**
5. **been**
6. **did**
7. **sit**
8. **write**
9. **now**
10. **two**

Write She had long ears.

19 CVC

a mix (one and multi-change)

Date: _____

Reading Score: __/20

1. soak
2. seek
3. meak
4. meal
5. mail
6. mate
7. mut
8. hut
9. jut
10. pup
11. chip
12. hip
13. hope
14. lope
15. load
16. lad
17. laid
18. thin
19. win
20. goat

Spelling Score: __/10

1. _____
2. _____
3. _____
4. _____
5. _____
6. _____
7. _____
8. _____
9. _____
10. _____

Star Words
(71 through 80)

1. **long**
2. **more**
3. **been**
4. **than**
5. **sit**
6. **write**
7. **two**
8. **did**
9. **down**
10. **now**

Read and picture this little story:

I can soak my feet in my big tub. But I can not soak my feet in my big boat. I can sink my teeth in my red meat. But I can not sink my teeth in my red goat.

20 CVC

a mix (one and multi-change)

Date:_____

Reading Score: /20

1. cake
2. road
3. tell
4. Rick
5. Mike
6. will
7. zeek
8. reach
9. coat
10. sill
11. beach
12. back
13. bake
14. moon
15. thud
16. shack
17. shin
18. pep
19. math
20. lob

Spelling Score: /10

1. _____
2. _____
3. _____
4. _____
5. _____
6. _____
7. _____
8. _____
9. _____
10. _____

Star Words
(71 through 80)

1. **sit**
2. **write**
3. **long**
4. **than**
5. **more**
6. **down**
7. **been**
8. **now**
9. **did**
10. **two**

Read and picture this little story:

Tom had been to the shop. Tom had been to the lake. Tom had been to the rock. But Tom had not been to the moon!

21 CVC a mix (multi-change)

Date:_____

Reading Score: __/20

1. chub
2. chip
3. shop
4. rock
5. wup
6. jail
7. weep
8. pope
9. whip
10. jazz
11. joke
12. lock
13. room
14. shock
15. mam
16. zoom
17. shock
18. wham
19. root
20. rock

Spelling Score: __/10

1. _____
2. _____
3. _____
4. _____
5. _____
6. _____
7. _____
8. _____
9. _____
10. _____

Star Words
(81 through 90)

1. **would**
2. **word**
3. **many**
4. **get**
5. **about**
6. **from**
7. **come**
8. **made**
9. **other**
10. **could**

Read and picture this little story:

Kim could come to Red Lake. She would come to Red Lake soon. She would not come to the other lake. She could not go that many miles.

22 CVC

Find the two nonwords in the list!

Date:_____

Reading   Score: /20

1. chill
2. fat
3. deep
4. dull
5. hup
6. fig
7. nope
8. whip
9. thug
10. zeal
11. sash
12. weep
13. sick
14. Nash
15. soak
16. Cate
17. pain
18. him
19. thin
20. zot

Spelling   Score: /10

1. _____
2. _____
3. _____
4. _____
5. _____
6. _____
7. _____
8. _____
9. _____
10. _____

Star Words
(81 through 90)

1. **many**
2. **made**
3. **get**
4. **would**
5. **could**
6. **other**
7. **from**
8. **word**
9. **come**
10. **about**

Read and picture this little story:

I could go. I would go. I should go. I will go to the moon.

23 CVC

Find the two nonwords in the list.

Date:_____

Reading Score: __/20

1. Pete
2. win
3. boat
4. miss
5. bell
6. cut
7. sim
8. home
9. lame
10. wait
11. week
12. weak
13. moon
14. vote
15. chib
16. zip
17. bath
18. noon
19. log
20. tin

Spelling Score: __/10

1. _____
2. _____
3. _____
4. _____
5. _____
6. _____
7. _____
8. _____
9. _____
10. _____

Star Words
(81 through 90)

1. **from**
2. **made**
3. **other**
4. **about**
5. **word**
6. **could**
7. **many**
8. **would**
9. **come**
10. **get**

Read and picture this little story:

He could see his mom. He would see his mom. He should see his mom. He did see his mom, and they had fun!

24 CVC

Find the two nonwords in the list.

Date:_____

Reading Score: /20

1. nine
2. heap
3. bath
4. keep
5. bog
6. moop
7. teeth
8. rash
9. booth
10. dome
11. pod
12. meeth
13. duck
14. mob
15. roof
16. fine
17. bib
18. pipe
19. meat
20. meet

Spelling Score: /10

1. _____
2. _____
3. _____
4. _____
5. _____
6. _____
7. _____
8. _____
9. _____
10. _____

Star Words
(81 through 90)

1. **word**
2. **many**
3. **come**
4. **would**
5. **could**
6. **from**
7. **made**
8. **get**
9. **about**
10. **other**

★ *Write* He could see his mom.

25 CVC

Find the two nonwords in the list.

Date:_____

Reading   Score: /20

1. zif
2. zap
3. bum
4. lame
5. rap
6. led
7. rell
8. soap
9. rate
10. nap
11. deck
12. dale
13. let
14. shale
15. muck
16. shot
17. run
18. read
19. fate
20. neck

Spelling   Score: /10

1. _____
2. _____
3. _____
4. _____
5. _____
6. _____
7. _____
8. _____
9. _____
10. _____

Star Words
(81 through 90)

1. **other**
2. **could**
3. **word**
4. **would**
5. **about**
6. **made**
7. **come**
8. **get**
9. **from**
10. **many**

Read and picture this little story:

Jill could write a word. She could write two words. She could write a lot of words. Jill could write about her dog and her duck.

26 CVC

Find the two nonwords in the list.

Date:_____

Reading Score: /20

1. math
2. chum
3. pass
4. cab
5. vibe
6. hish
7. cash
8. wish
9. lash
10. reach
11. dam
12. mog
13. fin
14. nail
15. sane
16. dig
17. game
18. rain
19. dog
20. ream

Spelling Score: /10

1. _____
2. _____
3. _____
4. _____
5. _____
6. _____
7. _____
8. _____
9. _____
10. _____

Star Words
(81 through 90)

1. **could**
2. **other**
3. **word**
4. **made**
5. **about**
6. **come**
7. **get**
8. **would**
9. **from**
10. **many**

Read and picture this little story:

Many times I would look at the moon. Many times I could look at the lake. Many times I could see the sun. Many times I had fun.

27 CVC

Find the two nonwords in the list.

Date:_____

Reading Score: ___/20

1. tag
2. joke
3. peach
4. roach
5. peash
6. five
7. load
8. bass
9. cod
10. loaf
11. chair
12. fish
13. wheat
14. deer
15. size
16. Ross
17. leaf
18. feep
19. dive
20. reach

Spelling Score: ___/10

1. _____
2. _____
3. _____
4. _____
5. _____
6. _____
7. _____
8. _____
9. _____
10. _____

Star Words
(81 through 90)

1. **about**
2. **from**
3. **many**
4. **word**
5. **could**
6. **get**
7. **made**
8. **would**
9. **come**
10. **other**

Read and picture this little story:

Dan had a word from his pal, Tom. Tom had a word from his pal, Kim, too. They both had pals. Now they are all pals.

28 CVC

Find the two nonwords in the list.

Date:_____

Reading Score: /20

1. hair
2. poach
3. wife
4. cuff
5. bell
6. hide
7. pape
8. sail
9. back
10. same
11. hop
12. them
13. seek
14. hoop
15. note
16. chain
17. lon
18. leap
19. bide
20. cad

Spelling Score: /10

1. _____
2. _____
3. _____
4. _____
5. _____
6. _____
7. _____
8. _____
9. _____
10. _____

Star Words
(81 through 90)

1. **get**
2. **made**
3. **from**
4. **could**
5. **come**
6. **about**
7. **many**
8. **other**
9. **word**
10. **would**

Read and picture this little story:

Could I get some food from you? Could I get some food from Mom too? Could I get some food from Dad too? If I do, I will be full and happy!

29 CVC

Find the two nonwords in the list.

Date: _____

Reading Score: ___/20

1. log
2. kiss
3. Shep
4. gale
5. ziz
6. roam
7. home
8. hug
9. but
10. came
11. mail
12. dug
13. goat
14. take
15. rack
16. tack
17. rake
18. hung
19. kid
20. soog

Spelling Score: ___/10

1. _____
2. _____
3. _____
4. _____
5. _____
6. _____
7. _____
8. _____
9. _____
10. _____

Star Words
(81 through 90)

1. **come**
2. **would**
3. **made**
4. **could**
5. **many**
6. **get**
7. **other**
8. **about**
9. **word**
10. **from**

Read and picture this little story:

There were many kids at the lake. There were many dogs at the lake. There were many cats at the lake. There were too many kids and pets at the lake.

30 CVC

Find the two nonwords in the list.

Date:_____

Reading	Score: /20	Spelling Score: /10	Star Words (81 through 90)

Reading Score: /20

- 1. Shane
- 2. yet
- 3. name
- 4. gath
- 5. shed
- 6. shine
- 7. bath
- 8. fail
- 9. wave
- 10. tell
- 11. wove
- 12. maid
- 13. zut
- 14. made
- 15. rode
- 16. hear
- 17. rang
- 18. lean
- 19. shut
- 20. tape

Spelling Score: /10

1. _____
2. _____
3. _____
4. _____
5. _____
6. _____
7. _____
8. _____
9. _____
10. _____

Star Words (81 through 90)

1. **made**
2. **about**
3. **many**
4. **would**
5. **get**
6. **come**
7. **could**
8. **other**
9. **from**
10. **word**

★ *Write* There were too many cats at the lake.

31 CVC

Find the two nonwords in the list.

Date: _____

Reading Score: /20

- 1. pit
- 2. sung
- 3. mean
- 4. got
- 5. van
- 6. thoop
- 7. gob
- 8. let
- 9. gave
- 10. luck
- 11. jug
- 12. beam
- 13. shame
- 14. bite
- 15. jam
- 16. jing
- 17. chip
- 18. feel
- 19. wheel
- 20. shin

Spelling Score: /10

1. _____
2. _____
3. _____
4. _____
5. _____
6. _____
7. _____
8. _____
9. _____
10. _____

Star Words
(a mix of 31-60)

1. **then**
2. **make**
3. **him**
4. **two**
5. **write**
6. **sit**
7. **did**
8. **other**
9. **would**
10. **could**

Read and picture this little story:

I had bad luck. I had a bite of jam on a chip. And a gob of jam got on my neck. It made a mess on my dress.

32 CVC

Find the two nonwords in the list.

Date:_____

Reading Score: /20

- 1. pet
- 2. jup
- 3. beer
- 4. fool
- 5. such
- 6. that
- 7. mill
- 8. hiss
- 9. lap
- 10. peep
- 11. moat
- 12. cheap
- 13. pipe
- 14. Dick
- 15. fizz
- 16. cool
- 17. bup
- 18. sheer
- 19. cute
- 20. mud

Spelling Score: /10

1. _____
2. _____
3. _____
4. _____
5. _____
6. _____
7. _____
8. _____
9. _____
10. _____

Star Words
(a mix of 61-90)

1. **word**
2. **now**
3. **more**
4. **some**
5. **her**
6. **long**
7. **than**
8. **has**
9. **time**
10. **been**

Read and picture this little story:

Dot is my sis. She has long red hair. She has long red nails. Now she has some red toes too.

33 CVC

Find the two nonwords in the list.

Date: _____

Reading Score: ___/20

_ 1. dot
_ 2. mass
_ 3. wib
_ 4. lush
_ 5. wet
_ 6. late
_ 7. bang
_ 8. much
_ 9. wail
_ 10. moat
_ 11. den
_ 12. buzz
_ 13. wooj
_ 14. June
_ 15. ripe
_ 16. nit
_ 17. sis
_ 18. fuzz
_ 19. hum
_ 20. whim

Spelling Score: ___/10

_ 1. _____
_ 2. _____
_ 3. _____
_ 4. _____
_ 5. _____
_ 6. _____
_ 7. _____
_ 8. _____
_ 9. _____
_ 10. _____

Star Words
(a mix of 61-90)

1. **these**
2. **look**
3. **from**
4. **down**
5. **like**
6. **made**
7. **get**
8. **about**
9. **many**
10. **come**

Read and picture this little story:

Jim can come to my home. He can look up and see my kite in the sky. He can look down and see my duck in the lake. We can look around and see it all.

34 CVC

Find the two nonwords in the list.

Date:_____

Reading Score: —/20

_ 1. deep
_ 2. cane
_ 3. ping
_ 4. roam
_ 5. thud
_ 6. wide
_ 7. haze
_ 8. tame
_ 9. rig
_ 10. weesh
_ 11. shave
_ 12. fate
_ 13. sheer
_ 14. lash
_ 15. pup
_ 16. jive
_ 17. mip
_ 18. fuss
_ 19. thug
_ 20. fun

Spelling Score: —/10

_ 1. _____
_ 2. _____
_ 3. _____
_ 4. _____
_ 5. _____
_ 6. _____
_ 7. _____
_ 8. _____
_ 9. _____
_ 10. _____

Star Words
(a mix of 61-90)

1. **made**
2. **than**
3. **down**
4. **from**
5. **word**
6. **make**
7. **time**
8. **these**
9. **then**
10. **about**

Read and picture this little story:

It is about time we got all done with these words. We have done a lot of work. We have done it all. We need to stop and have some fun!

Star Words 61-90

(61 through 70)	(71 through 80)	(81 through 90)
1. then	1. two	1. get
2. these	2. more	2. come
3. some	3. write	3. made
4. her	4. than	4. from
5. make	5. been	5. word
6. like	6. sit	6. other
7. him	7. did	7. about
8. time	8. now	8. many
9. has	9. down	9. would
10. look	10. long	10. could

Notes